THE SCIENCE OF

SOIL

Soil for Agriculture

REBECCA STEFOFF

Cavendish Square
New York

Published in 2017 by Cavendish Square Publishing, LLC
243 5th Avenue, Suite 136, New York, NY 10016

First Edition

Library of Congress Cataloging-in-Publication Data

Names: Stefoff, Rebecca, 1951-
Title: Soil for agriculture / Rebecca Stefoff.
Description: New York : Cavendish Square Publishing, [2017] | Series: Science of soil | Includes index.
Identifiers: LCCN 2016021846 | ISBN 9781502622259 (library bound) | ISBN 9781502622266 (eBook)
Subjects: LCSH: Soil conservation--Juvenile literature. | Soil management--Juvenile literature. | Agricultural conservation--Juvenile literature.
Classification: LCC S623.3 .S74 2017 | DDC 631.4--dc23

LC record available at https://lccn.loc.gov/2016021846

Editorial Director: David McNamara
Editor: Fletcher Doyle
Copy Editor: Rebecca Rohan
Associate Art Director: Amy Greenan
Designer: Stephanie Flecha
Production Coordinator: Karol Szymczuk

The photographs in this book are used by permission and through the courtesy of:
Cover Emily Suzanne McDonald/Blend Images/Getty Images; p. 4 bonzodog/Shutterstock.com; p. 6 Designua/Shutterstock.com; p. 8 Andrew Park/Shutterstock.com; p. 11 Omikron/Science Source/Getty Images; p. 13 Michal Szymanski/Shutterstock.com; p. 14 Martin Harvey/Photolibrary/Getty Images; p. 16 vainillaychile/Shutterstock.com; p. 18 Gary Cook/robertharding/Getty Images; p. 21 De Agostini Picture Library/Getty Images; p. 22 Maksim/File:ClaySumerianSickle.jpg/Wikimedia Commons; p. 23 Eliot Elisofon/The LIFE Picture Collection/Getty Images; p. 25 Alexson Scheppa Peisino/File:Pisac006.jpg/ Wikimedia Commons; p. 26 borsmenta/Shutterstock.com; p. 28 sybanto/Shutterstock.com; p. 32 Juan Silva/Photodisc/Getty Images; p. 35 Lisa F. Young/Shutterstock.com; p. 36 STR/AFP/Getty Images; p. 37 Yusnizam Yusof/Shutterstock.com; p. 38 Keith A Frith/Shuterstock.com; p. 42 Courtesy of NASA.

Printed in the United States of America

Contents

Along with flowers, this garden contains food plants, including tomatoes, peppers, and herbs.

1 From the Ground Up

Most of the food we eat comes from the ground in some way. Fruits, grains, nuts, and vegetables come from plants or trees that grow in the ground—or under it. Even the meat we eat comes from animals that eat plants.

Farming plants for people to use is called **agriculture**. The plants that are grown are called **crops**. How well those crops will grow has a lot to do with the **soil**.

The Earth's Skin

Soil is the top or outer layer of the Earth. It is like the skin of the planet. If the Earth were an orange, the soil would be the outside of the peel.

At times, soil is called by other names. Engineers and builders use the word "regolith." This is the mix of loose soil and small rocks that lies above solid rock.

Another common word is **dirt**. You might think that all soil is dirt, but dirt really means soil or earth that has been moved. If you dig a hole in the ground, the soil that you shovel out and toss to one side becomes dirt.

To the scientists who study rock and earth, the top layer of the Earth's surface is known as the **pedosphere**. It sits on top of the rocky shell they call the lithosphere.

Soil is not just the top layer of the Earth's surface—it can have layers of its own.

SOIL LAYERS

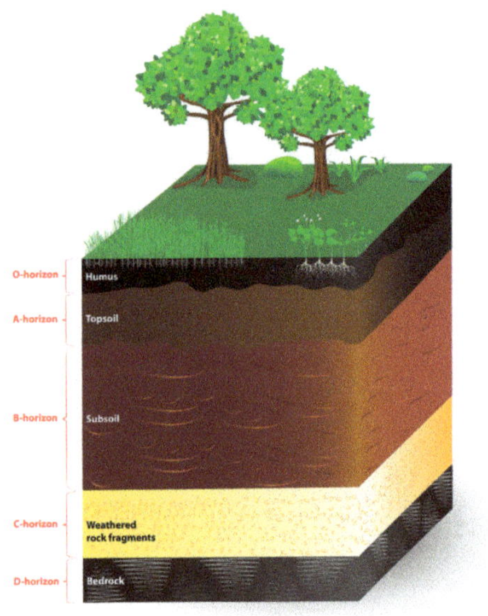

Five horizons, or layers, of earth. From top to bottom they are humus, topsoil, subsoil, weathered rock, and bedrock.

These layers of soil are sometimes called soil horizons. The top horizon is organic matter. It can be very thin. The next one is known as **topsoil**. This is the layer that gets moved when farm fields are plowed, and it is where most crops grow. Layers of soil under the topsoil are called **subsoils.**

Where Does Soil Come From?

Soil is a mix of earth, water, gases, dead plants, and tiny living things such as bacteria. The earth part of soil starts out as solid rock. **Weathering** makes it part of the soil.

Weathering is the breaking down of rock and earth into smaller pieces. This can happen in many ways. The word "weathering" is a clue—much of it happens because of weather.

Water gets into cracks in rock. When the weather turns cold, the water freezes into ice, which takes up more space than the water. The ice pushes against the rock, making the cracks larger. In time, the rock splits into chunks.

Wind causes weathering, too. It carries bits of sand or grit that can grind away at rock, turning it into powder. Rain and even air sometimes contain chemicals that cause weathering. A type of rain called acid rain contains chemicals from pollution. These chemicals eat away at stone.

Erosion is another name for some kinds of weathering. It is what happens when wind or water slowly wear away surfaces of rock or soil.

To make Arizona's Grand Canyon, the Colorado River cut through as much as a mile of rock.

The Grand Canyon shows what erosion can do. The canyon was created over millions of years by the Colorado River, which carved its path through many layers of rock. But erosion can also happen quickly. Floods in the Mississippi River can erode the river's banks, or wash them away, in just hours.

Weathering breaks solid rock into large boulders and then into smaller rocks. Over many years, weathering and erosion break those rocks into smaller and smaller pieces. First rocks become stones, then pebbles, then small pieces of gravel, and finally little grains of sand and tiny specks of earth. If the bits of sand and earth stay on land instead of being carried out to sea, they become part of the soil.

A World of Soils

There are many kinds of soil in the world. That is because different kinds of rock are broken down into soil. Not only are there many sources of soil material, but these

Gone with the Wind

Wind can be one of the most powerful forces on Earth. It can quickly turn farmland into dead fields. In the middle of the United States in the 1930s, erosion by wind created a wasteland called the Dust Bowl.

The Dust Bowl started when thousands of farmers planted wheat in the dry grasslands of Oklahoma, Texas, and other states of the Great Plains. To clear the land for wheat, the farmers plowed away the prairie grasses that had grown there for centuries with little rain.

At first, the wheat thrived, too. The farmers didn't know that the land had been getting more rain than normal from 1900 to 1930. Then less rain started falling each year. The rainfall was returning to normal—but the wheat farmers were caught off guard.

The year 1934 was very hot and dry. Crops withered and died in the fields. Without the thick prairie grasses

Towering clouds of dark, wind-blown soil sweep toward homes in the Dust Bowl of the 1930s.

and their web of roots, nothing held the soil in place. The wind carried it off in huge reddish-brown clouds. Some dust clouds traveled for days, choking cattle and blotting out the sun. New York City, Washington, DC, and even ships at sea were coated with fine, dry topsoil from the failed farms of the Dust Bowl.

By 1940, more than two million people had moved from the Great Plains because of the disaster that was the Dust Bowl. By the time the rain returned, the land had lost its best soil.

materials are moved from place to place by the forces that shape the Earth's surface.

Wind and water don't just erode rock and earth. They also carry pieces of rock and earth to new places. Rivers move soil over long distances. When a river floods, it can cause a lot of damage. However, it may also coat the land on either side of its banks with a layer of rich new soil.

Another kind of river also moves dirt and rock. A glacier is a slow-moving river of ice. Glaciers grind away at the ground. They push rocks and earth ahead of themselves, and they carry them along on their undersides. Glaciers have moved millions of tons of earth, a few inches at a time.

Fire can be a source of material for soil. Volcanoes spit ash, stones, and hot melted rock from deep within the earth. The ash can be carried great distances by the wind. The other materials flow down the sides of volcanoes. Later, weathering breaks them down and makes them

This huge boulder was carried to where it rests by the moving glacier behind it.

part of volcanic soil. The soil from volcanoes holds on to water but does not become soggy. This makes it perfect for growing coffee and grapes.

Just as weather changes from place to place in the world, soils are different, too. Long ago, ancient people learned to use different kinds of soil for agriculture.

A few groups of people in the world today still live by hunting and gathering wild foods.

2 Agriculture and History

In a few places today, people live by hunting and gathering. They hunt fish and animals for meat, and they gather wild food plants such as fruits. Everyone in the world used to live that way. Then some people started farming.

Over thousands of years, agriculture spread to most parts of the world. Everywhere that farming started, people had to learn how to use the soil.

The First Farmers

Scientists have found signs of ancient farms in the nations of Iraq and Iran in the Middle East. People there invented agriculture at least ten thousand years ago.

Not long after that, people in other parts of the world began farming. Centers of agriculture sprang up in Africa, India, China, New Guinea (a large island in Southeast Asia), Peru, and Mexico. From these starting places, agriculture spread across many lands.

Nobody knows exactly how farming got started. It probably happened as people gathered wild grains and other plant foods. The gatherers saw that these useful plants came back year after year in places where seeds had been scattered on the ground. The people started scattering seeds on purpose and digging holes in the ground to plant seeds.

The first crops in the Middle East were wheat, barley, peas, and tree-grown fruits such as figs. Farmers

Wild corn (maize) has much smaller cobs than modern domesticated corn.

grew rice in China and potatoes in Peru. Squash, corn, and beans were the main crops in Mexico.

Before long, farmers **domesticated** their food crops. This means that they chose seeds from their best plants, then planted those seeds. If they wanted taller grain or bigger apples, they used the seeds from the tallest grain and the biggest apples. Over time, domesticated grain, apples, and other crops became different from their wild cousins.

A New Way of Life

Agriculture brought a new way of life to ancient peoples around the world. Instead of moving around in small groups to look for food, people could grow food year after year in one place. They could settle down. Slowly, as farming took hold, camps grew into villages and towns.

Once people lived in settled communities, they could store more food because they didn't have to carry it around with them. They used pits, huts, and caves as **granaries**,

Early Native Americans built stone granaries such as this one to store harvested food.

places to store grain and other foods. This gave communities a supply of food to keep them going during hard times.

Agriculture meant that people could grow more food than they needed to feed themselves and their families. Not everyone had to be a full-time farmer. People could do other things. Some made pottery or tools. Other became soldiers or priests.

Communities grew into larger societies with different groups of people. The farmers paid taxes by giving a share of their crops to their leaders. This fed the merchants, armies, priests, and kings. Writing and numbers may have been invented to keep track of the crops and taxes.

Agriculture was a big part of trade between the peoples of the ancient world. More than 2,500 years ago, ships crossed the Mediterranean Sea carrying wine made from domesticated grapes. Ancient Rome collected shiploads of wheat from the lands it conquered in war.

The rise of farming led to the rise of civilizations in Asia, Africa, Europe, and the Americas. Along the way, farming changed. People learned more about how to use the soil.

Living on the Land

Early farmers soon realized that crops need good soil. Over the centuries, people around the world invented tools for working with soil. They also discovered new ways of using farmland. The oldest known farming tools are digging sticks and sickles.

Digging sticks were just what they sound like—long sticks with sharp ends that people used to dig holes for seeds. Later, with a small blade added to one end, the

The Gift of the Nile

Twenty-five hundred years ago, a Greek historian said that the civilization of Egypt was "the gift of the Nile." He meant that the Nile River brings two important things to Egypt's dry landscape. They are water and soil.

Ancient Egypt stretched for hundreds of miles along both banks of the Nile. Long before the people of Egypt built the mighty pyramids, they learned to use the river for agriculture. They counted on the Nile to flood every year.

The floods started in Ethiopia, a mountainous country south of Egypt. Every summer, heavy rains pounded Ethiopia's mountain slopes. This eroded the soil and washed it away. Floodwater full of soil entered the Nile, raising its level. Then it flowed north to Egypt.

By August, the high water reached Egypt. It overflowed the banks of the Nile into the farmers' fields. This did not harm the crops, because they had already been

The art of the ancient Egyptians shows them growing grapes and making wine.

harvested. The floods just gave the land a good soaking. In a month or two, the water level went down again. As the river sank back into its banks, it left Ethiopian soil on each side. The next year's crops were planted in this new layer of rich, moist soil.

The Nile has made farming possible in Egypt for more than five thousand years. Today, its flooding is controlled by dams, but it still brings the gift of life to a dry land.

stick became a hoe. Hoes are good tools for digging up the ground to plant seeds. They can also break up hard-packed soil and uproot weeds.

Sickles are curved blades that can cut through many stalks of grain in one swing. When a long wooden handle is added, a sickle becomes a scythe.

By four thousand years ago, people in the Middle East had invented the plow. This tool is a blade that is dragged through the ground. It makes a furrow—a line of turned-up soil ready to have seeds planted in it. With plows, people could move more soil, faster, than ever before.

Tools were not the only things that made farming easier. People also learned that certain ways of planting made the best use of their soil.

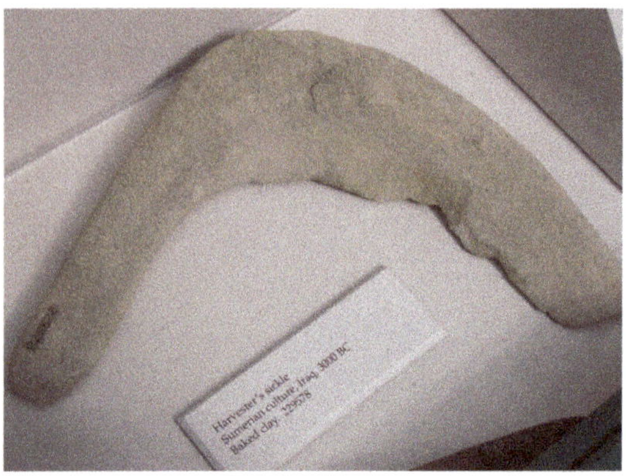

This sickle, used in the ancient Middle East to harvest grain, is made of baked clay.

All crops need at least some water. Some crops need a lot of water. However, not all soil is naturally wet. To grow crops in dry areas—even in some deserts—people used irrigation.

Irrigation means bringing water to where it is needed for farming. This is often done by digging canals or small

For thousands of years people have used simple pumps like this one in Africa to bring water to their fields.

channels to carry water from rivers and streams into farmers' fields. Machines called pumps can raise river water to the fields on the riverbanks. The ancient Egyptians made simple pumps that were buckets on the ends of poles. Farmers used the poles to lower the buckets into the river. They then swung the full buckets over to the fields and dumped the water into irrigation channels.

In China and other parts of Asia, people learned to farm rice in flooded fields called paddies. They built low walls of packed earth to hold shallow pools of water on the fields when the growing rice needed it.

Farming on steep hillsides was a challenge. Crops need water, but rain or irrigation could wash the soil downhill. People in many parts of the world solved that problem in the same way. They built terraces.

A terrace is a level patch built into a steep slope. The soil in the terrace is held in place by a wall, usually made of stones. Terraces are patches of farmland that

Centuries-old terraces let farmers grow crops on the slopes of Peru's Andes Mountains.

are protected from erosion. With terraces, people farm even on steep mountainsides.

Terraces save the soil. But what if the soil itself is not good enough for farming? People have come up with answers for that problem, too.

Two keys to successful farming are understanding and improving the soil.

3 Good Soil, Bad Soil

From damp rain forests to sandy deserts, the world has many kinds of soil. Some are better for agriculture than others. Farmers have ways to improve soil and make it more **fertile**, so that it will produce more or better crops.

Soil for Crops

Soil is a combination of four things. They are:

- **Minerals**. This part of soil comes from rock. It is made up of tiny pieces in three groups, based on their size. The largest pieces are grains of sand. The smallest pieces are clay. When dry, they are a fine powder. In between are medium-sized pieces, called silt.

Dead and decaying plant matter such as leaves and fallen trees is part of the soil's humus.

- **Water**. Soil ranges from very wet in damp forests to very dry in deserts. Even in deserts, though, soil usually contains a little water under the surface of the ground.

- **Air**. Soil has air in it because it is not solid. Air fills the tiny pockets between pieces of soil. Even far below the surface, soil contains some air.

- **Organic material**. Anything that is alive, or was once alive, is organic. Soil contains living things, such as plant roots, mushrooms, tiny bacteria, insects, and worms. It also contains humus, which is made when organic things die and decay. Fallen leaves, pine needles, dead plants, and even whole trees rot and break up into humus. So do dead animals. Nutrients from these things go into the soil as humus.

Different crops grow in different kinds of soil. Cabbages and broccoli can grow in soil with lots of clay. This kind of soil is sticky when it is wet. When it is dry, it splits and cracks. Potatoes and carrots can grow in sandy soil, which is loose and does not hold water very well.

Most crops grow best in a kind of soil that is called loam. The mineral part of loam is a blend of sand, silt, and clay. Loam has plenty of humus for nutrients, and it is good at holding on to water. Some loams are better for farming because of the chemicals in them. The chemical nitrogen, for example, is needed by growing plants. Soils without much nitrogen are not as fertile as soils with good nitrogen.

Hydrogen ions are also essential. Without hydrogen ions, plants can't absorb nutrients. Soil contains acid and alkaline. The balance between these two affects how many hydrogen ions the soil can attract. Soil pH measures this balance on a scale of 0 to 14. The lower the number, the more acid there is. The higher the number, the more alkaline there is. Soil with a rating of 7 is in perfect balance. The "p" in pH stands for potential and the "H" stands for hydrogen. The lower the number, the higher the potential for attracting hydrogen ions.

Of the seventeen essential plant nutrients, fourteen come from the soil. A soil pH of 6 to 7 is best for most nutrients. However, strong acid can hinder the bacteria that causes organic matter to decompose. When organic matter decomposes, it breaks down. When it breaks down, nitrogen and other nutrients are released into the soil. When it doesn't break down, the nutrients stay in the organic matter. This makes the soil less fertile.

Farmers keep track of soil pH to make sure it is in the range for best crop results.

Building Better Soil

A big part of agriculture has to do with trying to make bad soil good, and good soil better. There are ways to do this.

Soil stays healthier if it is not used in the same way all the time. Since ancient times, farmers have known that their soil is better if they let each field lie fallow once in a while. Fallow means not planting crops in a field for a year. This gives the soil a chance to rest. Fallow soil gets new nutrients from the weeds and wild plants that are left to decay on the land.

Soybeans *(foreground)* and corn *(back right)* grow side by side, restoring nutrients. The farmer may switch sides next year.

Another way to make soil better is crop rotation. This means growing different crops in the same field from year to year. One common form of crop rotation is to grow wheat in a field for one year, then use the same field to grow beans the next year. Another rotation is clover (used to feed livestock), followed by potatoes, followed by wheat. Some crop rotation plans use as many as six crops.

Crop rotation helps soil because different crops use different nutrients from the soil. The soil is not drained of a single nutrient season after season. Beans and peas are part of most crop rotations because bacteria that live on their roots take nitrogen from the air and add it to the soil.

Fertilizer can also make soil better for crops. A fertilizer is anything that people add to the soil to make it more fertile, or productive. Fertilizers contain nutrients that plants need. These nutrients are nitrogen, phosphorus, potassium, calcium, and more.

Some of the first fertilizers people used were manure and ashes. In the 1800s, scientists began making chemical fertilizers in factories. Today, many kinds of chemical fertilizers are used around the world.

The Green Revolution

Fertilizer played a big part in the Green Revolution. This was a new kind of agriculture that let people grow more food in their fields than ever before.

Try Working with Soil

You can learn about soil by growing plants in a small garden of your own. If you have a yard, see if there is a patch you can use. You don't need a yard, though. A window box or even a plastic pot or bowl will do, as long as it has small holes on the bottom so that water can drain out. Get an adult to help you find the things you will need.

Your first step is to make a layer of subsoil that water can trickle through. This will keep the roots of your plant from getting too wet, which can make them rot. Gravel or pebbles work well for this first layer.

On top of the subsoil, add a thicker layer of soil. You can take this from the ground, or you can buy planting soil or composting soil. If you use soil from the ground, make sure to break it up into small pieces. Take out any stones or sticks that might be in the soil. If the soil is

Placing soil in your pots in layers mimics conditions that would be found naturally in fields.

dry or light in color, you might want to add some fertilizer from a plant store.

Finally, plant something—a flower, or maybe an herb such as parsley to add to your food. You can plant either a few seeds or a young plant. Then, gently water your new garden. Make sure to keep it moist (but not dripping wet), and wait to see what happens.

The Green Revolution started in the 1940s. Scientists bred strains, or varieties, of wheat until they came up with a strain that had more grain on each stalk. They went on to do the same thing with rice and corn.

These new strains of wheat, rice, and corn came into use in many countries around the world. Where they were used, farmers produced more food. In the 1940s, the United States had to buy half of its wheat from other countries. By the 1960s, the Green Revolution had made the United States one of the world's top wheat growers. It sold wheat to other countries instead of buying it.

China, Mexico, and India were some of the other countries that grew much more food after the

Biologist Norman Borlaug received the Nobel Peace Prize in 1970 for developing food plants that brought about the Green Revolution.

This farmer is spreading fertilizer in a rice paddy. The Green Revolution crops need chemical fertilizers.

Green Revolution. The new crops saved millions of people from hunger or even starvation.

The new crops needed chemical fertilizers. Farmers had to use fertilizer year after year to grow as much food as possible on their land. The new crops also needed a lot of water.

The Green Revolution fed the growing number of people in the world. At the same time, it led farmers to stop growing older crops. Now much of the food in the world comes from just a handful of strains of wheat, corn, and rice.

A sample of soil is ready to be analyzed. Testing for nutrients is a major part of soil science.

4 The Future of Farming

Agriculture has shaped human society for at least ten thousand years. What does the future hold for farming—and for soil?

With a growing population, the world's need for food is growing, too. Some soil scientists are working to protect the soil that produces our food. Others are looking ahead to farming in the soil of other worlds.

Saving Our Soil

Soil can be destroyed much faster than it is made. It takes anywhere from one thousand to ten thousand years for nature to make a foot (30 centimeters) of soil. Erosion by wind or water can strip away that soil in a much shorter time. In just a few years, pollution from chemicals can ruin soil for farming. The loss of water can turn fertile farmland into a dry wasteland.

People and governments can act to make soil healthy and keep it that way. For example, there are ways to prevent erosion. One way is to not cut down all the trees and bushes on hillsides. Another is to plant borders of plants with sturdy root systems around fields, and leave them in place to help hold the soil. Another way is to build walls and terraces to slow the flow of water that carries soil away.

Some experts say that using fewer chemical fertilizers, weed killers, and **pesticides** on crops is good for the soil. Growing a variety of crops, not just one crop over a large area, also makes soil richer in nutrients.

Soil scientists are finding new ways to make soil more fertile without chemicals. Sometimes the answer is simple. In the Asian nation of Thailand, scientists tried adding clay to sandy soil. The clay helped the soil hold on to water and nutrients. Farmers who added the clay could grow more vegetables because their soil became healthier.

The Next Steps

In 2015, six astronauts on the International Space Station ate fresh lettuce with their packaged meals. They were the first people ever to eat food that had been grown in space.

Astronauts have grown food in space since the 1980s. Before 2015, the food was studied by scientists, not eaten. Now scientists know that healthy, safe food can be grown in space.

Some people dream of humans living in space. They might live in large space stations or ships that travel between the stars. Closer to home, companies and countries are thinking about building colonies on the moon or Mars.

Astronauts now eat fresh food grown in the space station. Future colonists may eat food grown on another world.

Feeding the people of any space colony will be a big challenge. For a colony to succeed, it will have to grow food. Scientists here on Earth have already started thinking about that challenge.

What would it take to turn Martian soil into farmland? Would humans have to carry humus and soil bacteria from Earth to Mars? Could they make fertilizer out of chemicals that are found on Mars? Someday, the first farmers on Mars may write a new chapter in the long story of people, food, and soil.

Glossary

agriculture Planting, tending, and harvesting crops.

crops Plants or fruits that are grown for human use.

dirt Earth or soil that has been moved.

domesticated Planted or tended by people; not wild.

erosion The wearing away of rock, soil, or other materials by wind, rain, or flowing water; one kind of weathering.

fertile Able to produce crops; full of the needed ingredients for agriculture.

fertilizer Anything that people put onto or into soil to make it more fertile or better for growing certain crops.

granaries Storage places for grain that has been harvested.

nutrients Substances that provide nourishment for growth, such as proteins and minerals.

pedosphere Scientific name for soil; or the thin, outermost layer of the Earth.

pesticide Something meant to protect crops from pests such as molds, insects, and mice.

silt Soil carried in water.

soil Top layer of the Earth's surface; a mix of loose earth, small rocks, gases, water, and tiny living things.

subsoils Layers of soil beneath the topsoil.

topsoil Top layer of soil, where most agriculture takes place.

weathering The breaking down of pieces of earth and rock into smaller pieces.

Further Information

Books

Graham, Ian and Mark Bergin. *You Wouldn't Want to Live Without Dirt!* Danbury, CT: Franklin Watts, 2016.

Rake, Jody S. *Roots, Bulbs, and Bacteria: Growths of the Underground.* Underground Safari. Minneapolis, MN: Capstone, 2015.

Reilly, Kathleen M. *Explore Soil: With 25 Great Projects*. Explore Your World. White River Junction, VT: Nomad Press, 2015.

Websites

Earth Science for Kids: Soil

www.ducksters.com/science/earth_science/soil_science.php

A page of facts about soil, with links to other pages on geology, the food chain, the nitrogen cycle, and more.

Growing a Nation: The Story of American Agriculture

www.agclassroom.org/gan/timeline/

This interactive timeline explores information about farming in the United States. It can be searched by decade or by topics such as "Farmers and the Land."

Index

Page numbers in **boldface** are illustrations. Entries in **boldface** are glossary terms.

About the Author

Rebecca Stefoff has written books for young readers on many topics in science, technology, and history. She is the author of the six-volume series Great Engineering (Cavendish Square, 2015), the six-volume series Is It Science? (Cavendish Square, 2014), and the four-volume series Animal Behavior Revealed (Cavendish Square, 2014). Her books for young people have also been published by Simon & Schuster, Seven Stories Press, Oxford University Press, and others. Stefoff lives in Portland, Oregon. You can learn more about her books for young people at www.rebeccastefoff.com.